BABY SHARKS

by Victor Gentle and Janet Perry

Gareth Stevens Publishing
A WORLD ALMANAC EDUCATION GROUP COMPANY

Please visit our web site at: www.garethstevens.com
For a free color catalog describing Gareth Stevens' list of high-quality books and
multimedia programs, call 1-800-542-2595 (USA) or 1-800-461-9120 (Canada).
Gareth Stevens Publishing's Fax: (414) 332-3567.

Library of Congress Cataloging-in-Publication Data

Gentle, Victor.
    Baby sharks / by Victor Gentle and Janet Perry.
        p. cm. — (Sharks: an imagination library series)
    Includes bibliographical references and index.
    ISBN 0-8368-2824-0 (lib. bdg.)
    1. Sharks—Infancy—Juvenile literature. [1. Sharks. 2. Animals—
Infancy.] I. Perry, Janet, 1960- II. Title.
QL638.9.G358 2001
597.3'139—dc21   00-052250

First published in 2001 by
Gareth Stevens Publishing
A World Almanac Education Group Company
330 West Olive Street, Suite 100
Milwaukee, WI 53212 USA

Text: Victor Gentle and Janet Perry
Page layout: Victor Gentle, Janet Perry, and Scott Krall
Cover design: Scott Krall
Series editor: Heidi Sjostrom
Picture Researcher: Diane Laska-Swanke

Photo credits: Cover, p. 15 © Mark Strickland/Innerspace Visions; pp. 5 (all), 11
© Mark Conlin/Innerspace Visions; pp. 7, 13, 19, 21 © Doug Perrine/Innerspace
Visions; pp. 9, 17 © Jeff Rotman/Innerspace Visions

Printed in the United States of America

1 2 3 4 5 6 7 8 9 05 04 03 02 01

Front cover: Adult and young silvertip sharks
are swimming together in the ocean to the south
of Thailand.

TABLE OF CONTENTS

The Case for a Few Sharks 4

That's No Yolk 6

It's an Inside Yolk 8

You're on Your Own, Kid 10

Hiding, Feeding, Growing 12

Beware of Other Sharks 14

Not Many Kids 16

A Long Time Growing 18

The Worst Danger of All 20

More to Read and View 22

Places to Write and Visit 22

Web Sites 23

Glossary and Index 24

Words that appear in the glossary are printed in **boldface** type the first time they occur in the text.

THE CASE FOR A FEW SHARKS

Even though every shark baby starts in an egg inside its mother, shark babies grow and get food in three different ways before they are born.

In some **species** of sharks, a strong egg case forms around the egg while it is inside the mother. Each egg case holds only one egg. After several days, the mother shark lays the egg case on the seabed. The unborn shark — the **embryo** — continues to grow. It feeds on the food stored in the egg **yolk**. It often stays in the egg for months before it finally hatches.

Sharks that lay eggs this way are called **oviparous**.

However, laying egg cases is not the most common way that sharks make more sharks.

A swell shark emerges from its egg case. As it swims away, it is on its own. Like all newborn sharks, this one has no parent to look after it.

THAT'S NO YOLK

Some shark embryos are fed in a totally different way. They stay inside the mother's body, and they get food straight from the mother.

For example, the embryos of hammerhead sharks, lemon sharks, and some other shark species get food this way. (It is similar to how mammals feed their embryos.) Instead of becoming an egg yolk that has food in it, the **"yolk sac"** attaches to the inside of the mother shark. Food then passes from the mother shark's blood to the baby.

Sharks whose embryos are fed this way are called **viviparous**. This is still not the most common way that shark embryos get food to grow on.

A live birth of a lemon shark. The newborn lemon shark leaves the mother, turns, and swims away.

IT'S AN INSIDE YOLK

The most common way for shark embryos to get food is also inside their mothers — but inside eggs that have egg yolks to feed the babies.

Most often, the embryos inside the eggs get all their food from yolk stored in a yolk sac in their eggs. No food passes directly to the babies from their mother's blood. The eggs hatch inside the mother. In some species, the strongest embryos feed on other eggs and other, weaker embryos inside the mother. Like viviparous sharks, these shark babies leave the mother when they are big enough to survive outside her body.

Sharks that grow their embryos in eggs kept inside their mothers are called **ovoviviparous**.

This is an adult velvetbelly lantern shark and an embryo with its yolk sac. This shark is a small, deep-water shark that glows in the dark. It grows to be about two feet (60 centimeters) long.

YOU'RE ON YOUR OWN, KID

Baby sharks have to take care of themselves as soon as they are born. Their parents don't stick around to protect them or feed them.

Most often, baby sharks are born (or hatch) in shallow waters. Here they will find plenty of seaweed, coral, rocks, or other hiding places. Baby sharks are often **camouflaged**. Their skin has colors and patterns that help the baby sharks hide in their surroundings.

Sometimes the biggest danger for baby sharks is a bigger shark. Even a baby that is born alive is ignored by its mother. She will not stay to protect it. Usually, she just swims away.

This newly hatched whitespotted bamboo shark is lying on its egg case. With luck, it will blend well enough into its background that it won't be spotted by a hungry **predator**.

HIDING, FEEDING, GROWING

Although there are dangers, most baby sharks are well equipped to handle them. In the early part of their lives, many sharks are camouflaged to help them hide in shallow areas. Here, among the plants and rocks, they find small creatures to feed on. Adult sharks usually stay in waters that are deeper than the waters where they grew up.

As young sharks grow, they may go into deeper, darker water. Often their baby coloring changes to hide them better in their new hunting grounds. Remember, they are not just hiding from their predators. Sharks also want to hide from their **prey** — the animals that the sharks are hunting.

This is a young tiger shark. Tiger sharks are ovoviviparous. They take about four to six years to grow big enough to have pups, and they have between 10 and 82 babies at one time!

BEWARE OF OTHER SHARKS

To survive, sharks need to eat, and they need to avoid being eaten (or killed for any other reason).

Almost any kind of sea creature can end up as shark food. In fact, sharks sometimes eat other sharks. Some will even eat other sharks of their own species, especially if these other sharks are hurt or caught in nets.

Many sharks, however, normally eat only certain types of food. Basking sharks and whale sharks eat mostly **plankton** (which are tiny plants, fish, and **crustaceans**). Other sharks are not so picky. Even if they do have a favorite fish dish, they will eat many other kinds of foods if they need to.

An adult and young silvertip shark are swimming together. This young shark is probably big enough to be safe from the adult — unless the young shark gets hurt.

NOT MANY KIDS

Shark babies, even cat shark babies, are called pups. Generally, sharks don't have many pups when they give birth.

Sand tiger sharks and mako sharks have only two pups in a **litter**. Basking sharks give birth to about six pups. Hammerhead sharks have some of the larger litters in the shark world — usually about forty to fifty pups at a time.

Sharks have much smaller litters than most other fish. Most fish lay thousands of eggs, but the **hatchlings** are usually small and defenseless. The tiny fish must find their own food immediately. Only a few of them will live. Most baby fish are eaten, or they starve when they float far from food.

These young scalloped hammerhead sharks are swimming at night near the Hawaiian Islands. Hammerheads often swim together in large and small groups.

A LONG TIME GROWING

Most sharks take many years to grow big enough to have pups. Six to ten years is not an unusual length of time, and some sharks take up to twenty years.

With so few baby sharks being born, and with many years to wait before they can reproduce, sharks must be well prepared to survive. Luckily for them, they are.

Whether they are oviparous, viviparous, or ovoviviparous, shark pups are born large and strong. They are ready to take care of themselves.

Most shark pups do grow up — or at least they did, in the times before humans hunted them so fiercely.

This blacktip shark is pregnant. Females must grow to about 5 feet (1.5 meters) before having babies. They carry the babies for 10 to 11 months before giving birth to 4 to 8 pups in a litter.

THE WORST DANGER OF ALL

Humans are the most dangerous predators that sharks have to face. Sometimes humans hunt sharks for their meat, their skin, and their oil. Humans also hunt and kill sharks just for the fun of it — for sport!

Today's shark species have survived for millions of years. In the last hundred years, humans have learned to kill sharks so fast and in such huge numbers that many shark species are in danger of being destroyed.

To save each rare shark species from becoming extinct — with none of that species left alive — people must hunt and kill fewer sharks.

Kitefin shark embryos and yolk sacs are piled in a garbage can at a shark processing plant on the Azores islands of Portugal. Overfishing has made this species very rare.

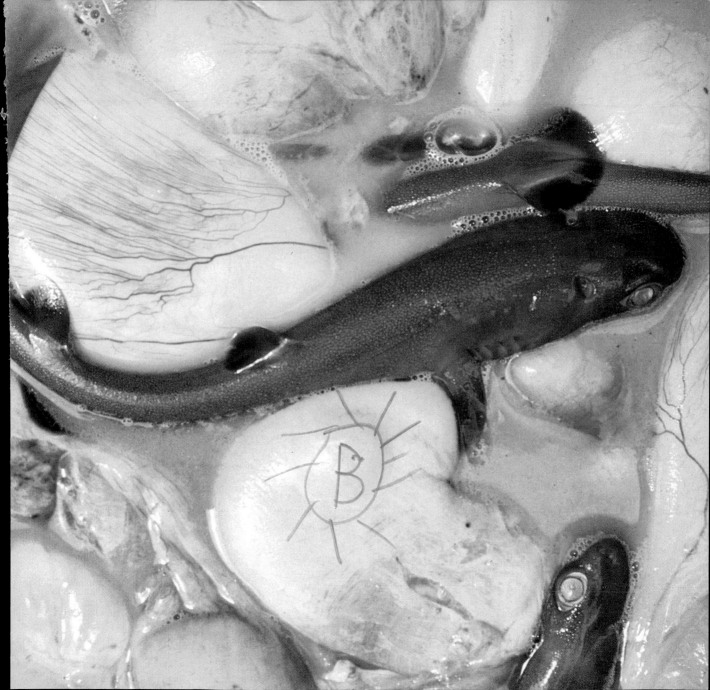

MORE TO READ AND VIEW

Books (Nonfiction)   *Outside and Inside Sharks.* Sandra Markle (Atheneum)
Sharks (series). Victor Gentle and Janet Perry (Gareth Stevens)
Tiburones/Sharks. Eyewitness Series in Spanish. Miranda MacQuitty
  (Santillana Publishing)
What Is a Fish? Science of Living Things (series). Bobbie Kalman and
  Allison Larin (Crabtree Publishing)
You Can Draw: Sharks, Whales, and Other Sea Creatures.
  Angelika Elsebach (DK Publishing)

Books (Fiction)   *The Great White Man-Eating Shark: A Cautionary Tale.* Margaret Mahy
  (Puffin) [also available in audio]
Shark Bite. Against the Odds (series). Todd Strasser (Minstrel Books)
Shark in School. Patricia Reilly Giff (Yearling Books)

Videos (Nonfiction)   *Eyewitness: Shark.* (Eyewitness)
National Geographic's Amazing Planet: Shark-A-Thon.
  (National Geographic)
National Geographic's Really Wild Animals: Deep Sea Dive.
  (National Geographic)

PLACES TO WRITE AND VISIT

Here are three places to contact for more information:

Greenpeace
702 H Street NW
Washington, DC 20001
USA
1-202-462-1177
www.greenpeace.org

World Wildlife Fund
1250 24th Street NW, Suite 500
Washington, DC 20037
USA
1-800-CALL-WWF
www.wwf.org

Vancouver Aquarium
P.O. Box 3232
Vancouver, BC
Canada V6B 3X8
1-604-659-3474

To find a zoo or aquarium to visit, check out **www.aza.org** and, on the American Zoo and
Aquarium's home page, look under AZA Services, and click on Find a Zoo or Aquarium.

WEB SITES

If you have your own computer and Internet access, great! If not, most libraries have Internet access. The Internet changes every day, and web sites come and go. We believe the sites we recommend here are likely to last, and that they give the best and most appropriate links for our readers to pursue their interest in sharks and their environment.

www.ajkids.com
This is the junior Ask Jeeves site — it's a great research tool. Some questions to try out in Ask Jeeves Kids:
> *Are some sharks like mammals?*
> *Why are baby sharks camouflaged?*
You can also just type in words and phrases with "?" at the end, for example:
> *Plankton?*
> *Mermaid's purses?*

kids.discovery.com/KIDS
Click on the Live SharkCam. See a live leopard shark and live blacktip reef sharks!

oberon.educ.sfu.ca/splash/tank.htm
It's the Touch Tank. Click on a critter or a rock in the aquarium to learn more about it.

www2.orbit.net.mt/sharkman.htm
Enter the Sharkman's World near Malta. He's a scuba diver who is completely soaked in anything even a little bit sharky. You'll find poetry, music, and shark pictures there. The Sharkman is not a scientist, but he loves to talk sharks with other shark fans — like you!

SharkCove.homestead.com/index.html
This is Shark Girl's page! This is a creative, informative, lively, and "100% kid safe" page created by an enthusiastic shark lover. Good graphics, amusing and educational sections, and good links are featured.

www.pbs.org/wgbh/nova/sharks/world/clickable.html
It's the Clickable Shark. Click on any part of the shark picture to find out how sharks work.

www.pbs.org/wgbh/nova/sharks/world/whoswho.html
Here's a shark "family tree." Click on any of the titles, and you'll see what kinds of sharks belong in the same group, and why. If you see a picture of a shark you don't know, use the Shark-O-Matic to get answers.

www.mbayaq.org/lc/kids_place/kidseq.asp
This is the Kids' E-quarium of the Monterey Bay Aquarium. Make postcards, print out coloring pages, play games, go on a virtual deep-sea dive, or find out about some marine science careers.

GLOSSARY

You can find these words on the pages listed. Reading a word in a sentence helps you understand it even better.

camouflaged (KAM-o-flahjd) — colored and patterned to blend with backgrounds 10, 12

crustaceans (krus-TAY-shuns) — animals that have gills and hard outer skeletons, like suits of armor, to protect their bodies 14

embryo (EM-bree-oh) — a baby animal that has not yet hatched or been born 4, 6, 8, 20

hatchlings (HACH-lings) — small, recently hatched creatures 16

litter (LITT-er) — all of an animal's young that were born at the same time 16, 18

oviparous (oh-VIH-par-us) — reproducing by laying eggs outside the body 4, 18

ovoviviparous (oh-voh-vih-VIH-par-us) — reproducing by giving live birth to young that eat yolk in eggs protected inside the mother's body until they hatch 8, 12, 18

plankton (PLANK-ten) — tiny animals and plants that drift in the ocean 14

predator (PRED-ah-ter) — an animal that hunts other animals for food 10, 12, 20

prey (PRAY) — animals that predators hunt for food 12

species (SPEE-shees) — a group of plants or animals that are like each other in many ways 4, 6, 8, 14, 20

viviparous (vi-VIH-par-us) — giving birth to live young that the mother's bloodstream has directly fed inside her body 6, 8, 18

yolk (YOKE) — the yellow, food-containing part of an egg 4, 6, 8, 20

yolk sac (YOKE SACK) — the thin-walled sack that usually contains the yolk 6, 8, 20

INDEX

camouflage 10, 12

egg cases 4, 10
eggs 4, 6, 8, 10, 16
embryos 4, 6, 8, 20
extinct 20

fish 14, 16
food 4, 6, 8, 12, 14, 16

hatching 4, 8, 10, 16
hunting 12, 18, 20

litters 16, 18

mammals 6
mothers 4, 6, 8, 10

oviparous 4, 18
ovoviviparous 8, 12, 18

plankton 14
predators 10, 12, 20
prey 12
pups 12, 16, 18

viviparous 6, 8, 18

yolk sacs 6, 8, 20
yolks 4, 6, 8, 20